Killing Memory,
Seeking Ancestors

Also by Haki R. Madhubuti

Claiming Earth: Race, Rage, Rape, Redemption
Blacks Seeking a Culture of Enlightened Empowerment
Black Men: Obsolete, Single, Dangerous? The Afrikan
American Family in Transition
From Plan to Planet: Life Studies: The Need for Afrikan Minds
and Institutions
Enemies: The Clash of the Races
A Capsule Course in Black Poetry Writing
(co-authored with Gwendolyn Brooks, Keorapetse
Kgositsile and Dudley Randall)

Poetry
Killing Memory, Seeking Ancestors
Earthquakes and Sunrise Missions
Book of Life
Directionscore: New and Selected Poems
We Walk the Way of the New World
Don't Cry, Scream
Black Pride
Think Black

Criticism
Dynamite Voices: Black Poets of the 1960's

Anthologies
Million Man March/Day of Absence: A Commemorative
Anthology: Speeches, Commentary, Photography,
Poetry, Illustration and Documents
(Co-edited by Maulana Karenga)
(Co-published with University of Sankore Press)
Confusion by Any Other Name: Essays Exploring the Negative
Impact of the Blackman's Guide to Understanding the
Blackwoman
Why L.A. Happened: Implications of the '92 Los Angeles
Rebellion
Say That the River Turns: The Impact of Gwendolyn Brooks
To Gwen, With Love (co-edited with Pat Brown and Francis
Ward)

Killing Memory, Seeking Ancestors

By Haki R. Madhubuti
(Don L. Lee)

Seventh Printing

Library of Congress Catalog Number: 85-82523
ISBN: 0-88378-093-3

THIRD WORLD PRESS
P.O. BOX 19730
CHICAGO, IL 60619

Cover design by Niki Mitchell

DEDICATION

Margaret Burroughs   Margaret Walker

Sterling A. Brown   Dudley Randall

Giants and Memory Makers All

IN REMEMBRANCE

Ella Baker
Maurice Bishop
Cheik Anta Diop
Bessie Head
Samora Machel
Alex La Guma
Bloke Modisane

they left large spaces

Contents

Prologue: Getting to This Place

I have had the privilege to travel far and deep into other cultures. Any kind of travel to the imaginative mind is both rewarding and challenging. Travel can also be painful to the culturally sensitive; for example, it is extremely difficult to enjoy oneself in Haiti and in certain parts of Afrika. Afrika entered my consciousness in 1960 and there has not been a day that I have not considered my relationship to that vast and complex continent.

I first went to Afrika in 1969 to attend the first Pan-Afrikan Festival in Algeria. After a decade of serious struggle in the United States for black self-determination, my visit to Afrika was crucial to my cultural development. I went looking for answers. The past ten years in the U.S. had been an intense period of struggle and study during which my generation fought to rid itself of a colonial-slave-centered mindset. My first trip to Afrika was instructive, but after seven visits to North, East and West Afrika, I am still fighting with my questions. My searchings have also taken me to the West Indies, Europe, Asia, and South America. However, as a man of Afrikan foreparents, the land of the sun has a special meaning for me.

Youth has its own naivety. I long ago lost my innocence in the concrete of Detroit and the mud of Arkansas. Yet, I was still not prepared for the land that gave birth to civilization.

My personal journals eat into my poetry. It is in poetry that I have learned to communicate best. I have become a poet, after fourteen books published in a twenty-one year period. I now feel comfortable with the description *poet* or *writer*. America has a way of forcing even the strongest into denying reality. Afrika demanded reentry.

In all of my work I've tried to give the readers melodies and songs that foster growth and questions. I wanted my readers to become a more informed and better people. I think that my experiences have made me a better person; I would like to think that I am a good and productive one also. That is partially what I am working for. Study, work, travel and struggle have taught me not to take myself too seriously, but to be serious enough so that others, especially my enemies, do not mistake love and caring for weakness.

Moving culturally from negro to Black to Afrikan to Afrikan American has been quite a trip. I *never* had to get "high" because my quest for knowledge (i.e., truth) carried with it a multiplicity of altitudes and attitudes. Progressive thinking and acting in most of the world can get one killed. This is what Afrika and Afrikan American struggle, in a highly abbreviated form, has taught me:

1. Before doing what I say, see what I do.
2. Good words are healthy, but deeds are what bring the food, clothe and house the children, and build tomorrows.
3. When one is full, it is easy to criticize the hungry.
4. It is easier to believe than to think.
5. What is increasingly rare among Western people is friend-ship and caring.
6. Honesty and moral consciousness practiced among the people has a greater impact than sharp-witted demagoguery.
7. Ideas run the world.
8. Force is both an idea and a reality.
9. Children first, which means that family is pre-children.
10. That which is truly valuable cannot be bought.
11. Freedom is only given to people who do not understand it.
12. Greed disguised as need is a great enemy.
13. Do not surround yourself with people who always say yes.
14. Knowledge is non-decaying food, and study brings a vast harvest to those who partake of it.
15. A people that runs from the truth will never know beauty and will sleep with lies.
16. The only ignorant question is the one not asked.
17. One's culture is one's life.
18. Values based upon tradition, reason and practice are not negotiable and memory is knowledge.

19. Listening is to learning as water is to life.
20. Seeking beauty in relationships is as life-giving as the juice of carrots and the morning sun.

There is much more, but let me stop here; brevity is respected.

I have acquired a health skepticism; however, as many can attest, it is still easy to get to my heart. What is missing among Afrikan American people is *vision*. Many of our people think and act in a way that is embarrassing to the normal mind. However, in much of the world, the abnormal still defines normality.

It is a 24-hour-a-day job to be a conscious Afrikan in America (or the world) where the mass media hourly project anti-Black images. This is why a people's culture is critical to its development. It was Long and Collier who stated in their book, *Afro-American Writing*, that "Definitions are increasingly important. The survival of culture—any culture—depends in large measure on the nature of its definitions of itself and of those aspects of life on which its survival depends: for example, what the past implies, what freedom means, who the enemy is. The literature of a culture is a totality of the definitions, a self-portrait of that culture. Knowledge of a literature, then, yields valuable insight into the culture that produced it."

We are summer-time people; therefore, it is not so odd that we act funny in this environment. However, the world is changing rapidly and we must ride with the tide as we try to humanize it. Question everything, study, study and study some more. Smile often, stay clean, and seek beauty. Try not to be judgmental and petty in your actions. As the brothers say, "Stay up," and I will add: Keep struggling; stay strong and aware, too. To kill the people's memory is to remove them from history and future, but when the people believe in and act positively and passionately on such beliefs, only their children and the land will live longer.

H.R.M.
September, 1986

"Today I have many things to do:
I must kill my memory to the last trace,
I must numb my soul into stone
I must find a way to go on living."

                                        Anna Akhmatova

"I can remember hearing all they said, their muttering protests, their
whispered oaths, and all that spells their living in distress."

                                        Margaret Walker

"Black love, provide the adequate electric
for what is lapsed and lenient in us now...
Black love, prepare us for interruptions;
assaults, unwanted pauses, furnish for leavings and
        for losses..."

                                        Gwendolyn Brooks

Who Owns the Earth?

Killing Memory
For Nelson and Winnie Mandela

the soul and fire of windsongs must not be neutral
cannot be void of birth and dying
wasted life
locked
in the path of vicious horrors
masquerading
as progress and spheres of influence

what of mothers
without milk of willing love,
of fathers
whose eyes and vision
have been separated from feelings of earth and growth,
of children
whose thoughts dwell
on rest and food and
human kindness?

Tomorrow's future rains in
atrocious mediocrity and suffering deaths.

in america's america the exictement is over
a rock singer's glove and burning hair
as serious combat rages over
prayer in schools,
the best diet plan,
and women
learning how to lift weights
to the rhythms of
"what's love got to do with it?"

ask the children,
always the children caught in the
absent spaces of adult juvenility
all

brake dancing and singing to
"everything is everything" while
noise occupies the mind as
garbage feeds the brain.

in el salvador mothers search for their sons
and teach their daughters the way of the knife.

in south afrika mothers bury hearts without bodies
while pursuing the secrets of forgotten foreparents.

in afghanistan mothers claim bones and teeth from
mass graves and curse the silent world.

in lebanon the sons and daughters receive horror hourly
sacrificing childhood for the promise of land.

in ethiopia mothers separate wheat from the desert's dust
while the bones of their children cut through dried skin.

tomorrow's future
may not belong to the people,
may not belong to dance or music
where
getting physical is not an exercise but
simply translates into people working,
people fighting,
people enduring insults and smiles,
enduring crippling histories and black pocket politics
wrapped in diseased blankets
bearing AIDS markings in white,
destined for victims that do not question
gifts from strangers
do not question
love of enemy.

who owns the earth?
most certainly not the people,
not the hands that work the waterways,

nor the backs bending in the sun,
or the boned fingers soldering transistors,
not the legs walking the massive fields,
or the knees glued to pews of storefront or granite churches
or the eyes blinded by computer terminals,
not the bloated bellies on toothpick legs
all victims of decisions
made at the washington monument and lenin's tomb
by aged actors viewing
red dawn and the *return of rambo part IX*.

tomorrow
may not belong to the
women and men laboring,
hustling,
determined to avoid contributing
to the wealth
of gravediggers from foreign soil
& soul.
determined to stop the erosion
of indigenous music
of building values
of traditions.

memory is only precious if
you have it.

memory is only functional
if it works for you.

people
of colors and voices
are locked in multi-basement state buildings
stealing memories
more efficient
than vultures tearing flesh
from
decaying bodies.

the order is that the people are to
believe and believe
questioning or contemplating
the direction of the weather is
unpatriotic.

it is not that we distrust poets and politicians.

we fear the disintegration of thought,
we fear the cheapening of language,
we fear the history of victims and the loss of vision,
we fear writers whose answer to
maggots drinking from the open
wounds of babies
is
to cry genocide while demanding
ten cents per word and
university chairs.
we fear politicians
that sell coffins at a discount
and consider ideas blasphemy
as young people world over bleed from the teeth while
aligning themselves with whoever
brings the food.
whoever brings love.

who speaks the language of
bright memory?

who speaks the language of
necessary memory?

the face of poetry must be fire erupting volcanoes,
hot silk forging new histories,
poetry delivering light greater than barricades of silence,
poetry dancing, preparing seers, warriors, healers
and parents beyond the age of babies,
poetry delivering melodies that cure dumbness & stupidity
yes, poets uttering to the intellect and spirit,

screaming to the genes and environments,
revitalizing the primacy of the word and world.
poets must speak the language of the rain,
    decipher the message of the sun,
    play the rhythms of the earth,
    demand the cleaning of the atmosphere,
    carry the will and way of the word,
    feel the heart and questions of the people
    and be conditioned and ready
    to move.

to come
at midnight or noon

to run
against the monied hurricane in this
the hour of forgotten selves,
forgiven promises
and
frightening whispers
of rulers in heat.

The Union of Two
For Ife and Jake

What matters is the renewing and long running kinship
seeking common mission, willing work, memory, melody, song.

marriage is an art,
created by the serious, enjoyed by the mature,
watered with morning and evening promises.

those who grow into love
remain anchored
like egyptian architecture and seasonal flowers.

it is afrikan that woman and man join in smile, tears, future.
it is traditional that men and women share expectations, celebrations,
    struggles.
it is legend that the nations start in the family.
it is afrikan that our circle expands.
it is wise that we believe in tomorrows, children, quality.
it is written that our vision will equal the promise.

so that your nation will live and tell your stories accurately,
you must be endless in your loving touch of each other,
your unification is the message,
continuance the answer.

August 7, 1986

Possibilities: Remembering Malcolm X

it was not that you were pure.
your contradictions were small wheels,
returning to the critical questions:
    what is good?
    what does it mean to be black?
    what is wise?
    what is beautiful?
    where are the women and men of honor?
    what is a moral-ethical consciousness?
    where will our tomorrows be?
    what does a people need to mature?

it was your search and doings
that separated you from puppets.
"a man lives as a man does"

if you lived among the committed
this day how would you lead us?

what would be your strength,
the word, the example, both?

would you style in thousand
dollar suits and false eye glasses?

would you kneel at the feet of arabs
that raped your grandmother?

would you surround yourself with
zombies in bow ties, zombies with parrot tongues?

it was not that you were pure.
the integrity of your vision and pain,
the quality of your heart and decision
confirmed your caring for local people, and your
refusal to assassinate progressive thought
has carved your imprint on the serious.

Aberrations

hair, color and quiet desperation in the last quarter of the
20th century.

post-1986 and it is still political to, consciously or unconsciously,
desire hair that is straight or curly in the fashion of europe
and to seek the lightest and "fairest" of people to love while
proclaiming one's deepest and undying commitment to all that is
black, and on paper, beautiful.

the utter pain of being dark
and women,
living among men who despise
the "nappiness" of head & the
hue of skin sunbaked before birth.

the unimaginable hurt of being dark
and short and man,
living among images of vikings
tall and conquering
"angel-like" roaming the earth
seeding the wombs of the vanquished coloreds.

the war was fought
when being natural became anti-self & unkind,
the war was confusing
when we lied to ourselves to convince
the nonbelief in us,
the war was in disorder
when practice became embarrassing,
the war was lost
when self-hatred emerged as a force greater than the
scorn of sworn enemies.

beauty and being beautiful is not the question.
all people desire beauty.
a full people needs love,
music and flowers in their lives.

whose love remands the answer?
whose music determines the call?
whose beauty decides the winner?
whose culture dictates the dance?

what is the color and texture of your flower?

The End of White World Supremacy

The day, hour, minute
and
second that the
chinese
and
japanese
sign
a
joint
industrial
and
military
pact.

In Moonlight and After

Searching

1. Sisters

in moonlight and after
beautiful women speak in tongues and
answers.

where is the music?
where is the passionate fire promised?
running
with the men—loudly,
backward and fisted
fastly and crudely becoming the
enemy of silence,
enemy of love and vision.

friend of despair and destruction
tonight and often
many and more of the womenblack are
alone
and searching with children
some
creating networks of hatred
for the limitations in their lives
robbed of laughter and joy
challenged by biology and babies
as the men
keep company with others and themselves.

2. Empty warriors

the men,
occupying bedrooms and unemployment lines, on corners, in bars,
stranded between middle management and bankruptcy, caught in
warped mindsets of "success in america," the kind taught to
first generation immigrants at local trade schools and jr.
colleges, taught to people lost and unaware of history or
future, ignorant of the middle passages.

the men,
occupying space with men and motives, in prisons, in safe
houses, shooting up with juice and junk, many with hairless
noses and needle-marked toes, searching for missing history,
searching for the when and how of "making it in america,"

the men
escaped and taken, twice and three times absorbed in life and
sharing, absorbed in locating the mission and magic, the manner
and muscle, the answer and aims, walking the borders between
smiles and outrage.

3. Transitions

in moonlight and after,
beautiful women,

respected women become elders of the storm,
riders of the hurricane,
keepers of the volcano,
warm and worked,
caught and embittered
often blaming
themselves for misery planned before their birth,
for hurt conceived by slaveholders on wall street,
executed prior to foreparents' arrival to consciousness.

4. Arrivals

of the women clean and cured,
of the men sensitive and sound,
all focused and calm,
listeners of a distant wind
love full and wanted
they
did not wait
& knew in the aloneness of early hours
that
snow was temporary and transient
    understood that evil could not be conquered
    on knees with folded hands,
    understood that ten decades of
    colorless rice, enriched bread and sugar
    would weaken a people,
    understood too that slavery, if it is to work,
    has to be accepted by the enslaved.
snow is temporary and heat does boil water.

5. The gathering

gathering as they do with
their water and weather,

their heat and blankets,
their thoughts and hearts,
wrapping their children and songs
in the mysteries of their men being butchered
beyond recognition.
some rushing
to the wilderness of
urban consumption and corporate takeovers,
in the midnight of a wasted culture of pornographic values,
in the indecisions of life and loving.
others coming with care
seeking
quality in the confusion of mistaken loyalties,
demanding
quality of responses,
quality in the searching,
quality in the giving and loving,
quality in the receiving
beginning anew.
   fresh.

POET: Gwendolyn Brooks at 70

as in music,
as in griots singing,
as in language mastered, matured
beyond melodic roots.

you came from the land of ivory and vegetation,
of seasons with large women guarding secrets.
your father was a running mountain,
your mother a crop-gatherer and God-carrier,
your family, earthgrown waterfalls,
all tested, clearheaded, focused.
ready to engage.

centuries displaced in this land of denial and disbelief,
this land of slavery and sugar diets,
of bacon breakfasts, short suns and long moons,
you sought memory and hidden ideas,
while writing the portrait of a battered people.

artfully you avoided becoming a literary museum,
side-stepped retirement and canonization,
gently casting a rising shadow over a generation of
urgent-creators waiting to make fire,
make change.

with the wind in your hand,
as in trumpeter blowing,
as in poet singing,
as in sister of the people, of the language,
smile at your work.

your harvest is coming in, bountifully.

Magnificent Tomorrows

For Queen Mother Moore, Karima White, Sonia Sanchez,
Mari Evans, Ruby Dee, Assata Shakur, Julia Fields, and Janet Sankey

1.
flames from sun
fire in during rainbow nights.

the women are colors of earth and ocean—
earth as life,
the beginning waters,
magnificent energy.

as the women go, so go the people,
determining mission,
determining possibilities.

stopping the women stops the future.
to understand slavery, feel the eyes of mothers.
there lies hope of destruction, lies unspeakable horror or
fruitful destiny.

we
are now in the europe of our song,
non-melody with little beat or hope.
current dreams are visionless,
producing behavior absent of greatness.

2.
without great teachings,
without important thoughts,
without significant deeds,
the ordinary emerges as accepted example
gluing the women
to kitchens,
afternoon soaps,
and the limiting imagination of sightless men.
producing
a people that move with the
quickness of decapitated bodies
while
calling such movement
divine.

possibilities: listen to the wind of women, the voices of big
mama, zora neale, sister rosa, fanny lou, pretty renee, gwen brooks,
queen nzinga, and warrior mothers. all birth and prophecy, black
and heart warm, bare and precise. the women detailing the coming
collapse or rise. the best and bent of youth emerging. telling
triumphantly. if we listen, if we feel & prepare.

3.
if black women do not love,
there is no love.
if black women do not love,
harmony and sustaining humanity cease.
if black women do not love,
strength disconnects.
families sicken, growth is questionable &
there are few reasons to conquer ideas or foe.

as black women love
europe gives way to southern meals,
as black women mature,
so come flames from sun,
rainbows at dusk,
sculpture of elizabeth catlett and
music of nina simone.
as womenblack connect,
the earth expands, minds open and books reveal the possible
if we study
if we feel the flow & secrets of our women,
if we listen,
if we concentrate,
if we carefully care,
if we simply do.

Always Remember Where You Are
For Zora Neale Hurston

1.
it seems as though she had been
planted outside northwestern high
next to the basketball court on 86th street
behind her weather worn blue buick
seated on a rusting folding
chair where she sold cookies, candies, history,
causes, chewing gum, vision, corn chips,
soda pop and advice to teenagers with
26-year-old mothers and grandmothers
under 40. most of their fathers music
ceased during viet nam and the f.b.i.'s
war against black men who dared to
question the saintliness of congress and the
imperial presidency.

2.
She sold wisdom from her weather
worn buick bought for her by her son,
a former NBA basketball star. he had
earned NBA records and money in new york
during the 60s and 70s flying high above
hoops and reality only to slip on a
nickel bag and later fall into deadly
habit of sniffing his breakfast, lunch
and dinner. eventually his snacks interrupted
practice and games as his place in
the world became that of a certified
junky circling a basketball that
he could not bounce and a mother
he could not recognize, nor she him.

3.
As his records faded and his money
disappeared quicker than shit in
a flushing toilet, he returned home to
mamma, a pitiful casuality, unable
to write his name or remember the
love that got him out of dusable high
with scholarship offers from 50
universities, no questions asked.
that his mother cared and he was 1st team
all american high school and college is
now history. this mother, in the august
and winter of her time, with eyes
and smile frozen in urban memories,
sells sugar and dreams now from the
trunk of destroyed promises in america.

Poem Resulting from a Television Ad
For *The Color Purple*

Girl
"you sho is ugly,"
broken too,
auctioned off.
sold and resold again & again
prostituted by
negroes passing & modern slavemasters
who smell gold,
smell VCR royalties,
smell cable TV rentals,
smell negroes willing to kneel, and suck again.

knowing that women "ugly" and non-ugly, "dumb" and undumb,
    daily at
typing pools, day-care centers, laundrymats, card parties, avon
    lunches,
factory assembly lines and tupperware picnics share horror
    stories of
their lives with men and will dress in sunday's best to stand in
    minus 14
degree wind chill premiers to see themselves beaten and
    humiliated to
confirm fact and rumor of rough life and the insightfulness of
    d.w. griffith's *birth of a nation.*

the women of good words,
the women of history and content,
the women of balance,
the women who enjoy their men
are either lucky, lying or crazy.

lucky?
these women knew that black people didn't walk on water or
    come to
america first class twa.
to be in america is not luck but is a
little told chronicle of continental rape and hate.

lying?
the lie that america was bought
from indians on the trail of 1000 tears & that
colored people loved plantation life and
trees exist to hang black men from regardless of the
utterings of amos & andy, stepin fetchit and quincy jones.

crazy, black people who refuse to mentally die
or buy are crazy. elijah muhammad, martin luther king,
malcolm x were complete aberrations & crazy.
crazy. paul robeson, triple crazy.
harriet tubman, fannie lou hamer, southern crazy.
marcus garvey, edward blyden, claude mckay
south of florida caribbean crazy.
margaret danner, larry neal, hoyt w. fuller, literary crazy.
bob marley, bessie smith, marvin gaye,
musically, musically crazy, crazy before contact with europeans
    crazy,
black people who refuse to mentally
die or buy into america's
nightmare are positively
crazy.

Woman with Meaning

she is small and round,
round face and shoulders connected to half-sun breast,
on a round stomach that sits on rounded buttocks,
held up by short curved legs and circular feet,
her smile reveals bright teeth, and when it comes,
her eyes sing joy and her face issues in gladness,
she is brilliant beauty.

she likes colors,
her hair, which is worn in its natural form, is
often accented with vivid, cheerful scarfs. her make-up
is difficult to detect, it complements her oak colored skin,
suggesting statuesque music. her scent is fresh mango
and moroccan musk. her clothes are like haitian paintings,
highly noticeable during her rhythmic walks,
as she steps like a dancer.

she is a serious woman,
her values,
her ideas,
her attitudes,
her actions are those of a reflective mind.
her child is her life,
her people their future,
she and her child live alone and the brothers
speak good words about them.

the brothers,
married and unmarried, want to help her.
it is difficult to be with her and not
lose one's sense of balance,
one's sense of place and wisdom.
that is what caring does.

her aloneness
hurts and tears at the inside of serious men.
some of the older men have tried
to tie her heart into theirs but
the commitment was never enough.
her sense of honor and history,
her knowing of sisterhood and rightness
force her to sleep alone each night.

the brothers
continue to speak good words about her,
many
when thinking of her smile.
others light candles and pray.
some send her notes, gifts and poems,

all
hoping for the unexpected.

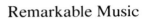

Remarkable Music

Question: What Is the Greatest Challenge
You Face as a Black Man?

Answer: My continued quest is to be a responsible, loving and effective Black man, husband, father, writer, educator and publisher in this ocean of *white world supremacy* (racism), and not to allow *white supremacy* to alter or destroy my memory, spirit, drive, integrity, worldview, convictions and values, that are the results of twenty-five years of work, excruciating pain, serious study, critical thinking—actions and organized struggle.

Also, with my wife, my challenge is to pass on to our children positive Afrikan (Black) values; which demand the maintenance and development of our family, extended family, community, and people, by highlighting and pushing progressive ideas as well as historical examples of Harriet Tubman, Nat Turner, Martin R. Delaney, Marcus Garvey, Mary McLeod Bethune, Fannie Lou Hamer, Martin Luther King, Malcolm X and others.

My fight is to be an inspired example of a caring, healthy, intelligent, and hard working brother who understands this *war* and works daily for the development of our brothers into multi-talented, family-based, conscientious Black men who will not settle for anything less than self-determination and beauty for all people.

Hoyt W. Fuller: No Easy Compromises

There is something magical about a person who has a passion for ideas. A part of the magic is that he or she is usually very serious and is a person with high standards and a definable purpose for living that is far beyond the ordinary. If such a person is willing and able to share his love — and in doing so, change others for the better — he needs to be remembered. Hoyt W. Fuller lived ahead of his time and, as is often the case of visionaries, he was impatient with mediocrity and ignorance. Yet, within the imperfections of growing up in America, he shared his music and mission with us to the end of his bright and influential life.

Hoyt Fuller's work influenced a generation of young scholars, activists, poets, teachers, writers and thinkers. His voice, quiet and consistent as editor of the important *Black World* (*Negro Digest*) and *First World* magazines, introduced Afro-American and African literature and writers to an international audience. His book, *Journey to Africa*, set the tone for a serious consideration and contemplation of that massive and complex continent. As teacher (adjunct professor at Northwestern and Cornell universities) and editor, he brought clarity to the turbulent decades of the Sixties and Seventies. True to the music of his time, he was the melody rather than the rhythm. His voice was direct and served as a roadmap for millions. He detested confusion in thought or language.

The quality that impressed me the most about Mr. Fuller was the maturity and thoughtfulness of his responses. It seemed as though most of his answers were logical and consistent with his actions. He seldom spoke from the top of his head and was Black (culturally, consciously, and in color), before it was popular, and always in an instructive and non-dogmatic manner. There was a hard morality to his presence without the self-righteousness. He represented that which was decent, human and right in this world. Mr. Fuller was a true lover of life and words. He travelled among many languages and cultures and was an emotionally voracious reader of international literature.

The pronoun "I" seldom cluttered his lexicon, and his sense of *style* was in the league of Duke Ellington and Gwendolyn Brooks. He took on the bullies of the world using carefully structured sentences that displayed educated urban metaphors, exemplifying a serious mind at work. He exhibited preparedness and winning possibilities. His dedication to young writers and creators helped to launch hundreds of poets, essayists, playwrights, novelists, visual artists, photographers and thinkers into the international arena. Hoyt Fuller was a "cultural" father to an entire generation of Black word-users. His uncompromising mind, his magic and music are missed. Few are able to sing his songs.

"compared to what," goes the song.
try example and originator.
try man of memory and legacy,
        man of destiny and future.
earthly visitor and runner among us,
suggesting *words* as mode and form,
        language morally precise,
demanding literacy and enlightenment,
as the ingredients for
beauty,
wisdom.

First World
For Cheikh Anta Diop

We were raised on the lower eastside of detroit,
close to harlem, new york, around the block from watts,
next to the mississippi delta in north america.
unaware of source or history, unaware of reasons,
whys, or beginnings. accepting tarzan and she woman,
accepting kong as king, accepting stanley—livingstone and
europecentric afrika, accepting british novels, french language
and portuguese folktales that devastated afrika's music & magic,
values and vision, people.

you helped restore memories,
gave us place and time,
positioned us within content and warnings,
centered us for the fire from the
first world:
original at dawn, founder of knowledge, inception. definer.
center of life, initial thinker, earliest, earliest order.
primary and wise, foremost, predominantly black, explainer,
mature pioneer, seer, roundrooted, earthlike, beginning tree,
cultivator, sourcegiver, genesis, entrance, tomorrow's light.
vision, unarguably afrikan.

Remarkable Music and Measure:
Remembering the Fathers and the Sons

For Chancellor Williams, Ossie Davis, Yosef ben Jochannan,
Hoyt W. Fuller, John H. Clarke, and Hannibal Tirus Afrik

these men
are alive & doing in this world.
all find the mediocre depressing and stimulating.

they function on sun & moon & mission.
their energy seldom dances within the
debilitating sight of others.
their expectations represent great challenge, clear motivation.

large moments exist between talkers and doers,
between original and carbon,
between infantile showboats and producers of brilliant
    tomorrows.

these men take the negative and create winning potentialities,
confronting fears
and discouraging the gossip of fools or foe,
discouraging smallness in all.

their women are remarkable music and measure,
bright desert dust, rugged fruit bearers,
expectors, of clear options and family-first,
anticipating men, answers, results.

magic of the dark spirit guides them
over the dirt of europe and votive of afrika,
equipping them to recognize the enemy, whether barbarians,
priests or cabinet members in the government of assassins.

they understand the failure we strap to our own dreams.

as others & most do the robot,
they compose new melodies and
choreograph the warrior's prayer.

rulers and leaders,
followers of demagogues and noise makers
with brains of floating rocks forever seek them out.

not born great,
they decided early not to swim in the
butt prints of others

selecting to conquer ignorance and evil,
selecting to run with ideas as others and many
knee-danced and drove mercedes over the rainbows of our
    children.

not born great,
they caused confusion in the tower,
worried captains of gun ships and
left large plants on this earth.

born like us, bronze and promising,
able to laugh and refuse greed in the wheat while
rejecting fairy tales and fashions from europe.

they are better, best and remarkable.
the measure of their music
is that certified fools and clowns
act intelligent in their light.

Moving to the Next Moment
For James Turner & Family

our caring comes in the light,
in the quality of your responses.

our caring from ocean to inland reflects
the influence of your doings and utterances.

rejecting retarding neutrality
you united blood and kin to:
     music and mission.
     loneliness of ice and distance,
     quest of melody and vision,
     bloodboldness and firstfind.

in you
our future continues,
our memories are secure and renewing,
our tomorrows certain and coming,
our expectations confirmed and connected.

bonded in the mind of a maturing people.

Honest Search
For Bobby Wright

with a mind as fast as a race track,
no wonder you were always running.

concerned about a people unaware of their own promise.

concerned about an answerless leadership lost
in material, status, pleasure acquisition

you did not dishonor the world, word or vision:
a fighter within the eye of the volcano,
a listener in the midst of the hurricane,
a lover unafraid of giving tears or laughter,
a scientist seeking bright and moving moments,
a deliverer of truths within the truths,
a tree rooted in history, beauty, permanence.
a good and honest man,
carrying wisdom.
carrying future.

we did not recognize greatness among us.

Moves

For Wilson Goode

a negro playing mayor and hardball,
playing dirty harry and the buck stops here,
forgot where he came from with an eye on
where he is,

forgetting the children dark,
the women black,
the men afrikan,
whose hair, diet and ideas clashed with
where they and he are.

in the city of bells and love
for certain brothers,
a negro
plays white and mayor,
makes history in america
by disregarding the bill of rights
while dropping bombs on
who he used to be.

confirming and confirming
that america is still number one
in the manufacturing of
niggers.

Pollution: Part 1

a former jazz singer and
sideman to an imitation tap dance team,
recognizing his mediocrity
as a professional entertainer,
decided to use his gifts
in an area where competence is
uneven, less taxing and not measured
by melody or footmanship.

our singer-dancer
possessing the looks women adored,
having the rap men appreciated,
being the color negroes wished for,
endowed with the hair babies are born with,
insightful enough to peep the weaknesses
of his people,
changed his profession.

wilbert smith—
all 5′ 11″ of him—found a new name,
tailored his shirts,
bought a D.D. from a west coast jr. college,
picked up the
"most circulated book in the western world" and
    found god.

Poet: What Ever Happened to Luther?

he was strange weather, this luther. he read books, mainly poetry
and sometimes long books about people in foreign places. for a
young man he was too serious, he never did smile, and the family
still don't know if he had good teeth. he liked music too, even
tried to play the trumpet until he heard the young miles davis. He
then said that he'd try writing. the family didn't believe him
because there ain't never been no writers in this family, and
everybody knows that whatever you end up doing, it's gotta be in
your blood. It's like loving women, it's in the blood, arteries and
brains. this family don't even write letters, they call everybody.
thats why the phone is off 6 months out of a year. Then again, his
brother willie T. use to write long, long letters from prison about
the books he was reading by malcolm x, frantz fanon, george
jackson, richard wright and others. luther, unlike his brother,
didn't smoke or drink and he'd always be doing odd jobs to get
money. even his closest friends clyde and t. bone didn't fully
understand him. while they be partying all weekend, luther would
be traveling. he would take his little money with a bag full of
food, mainly fruit, and a change of underwear and get on the
greyhound bus and go. he said he be visiting cities. yet, the real
funny thing about luther was his ideas. he was always talking
about afrika and black people. he was into that black stuff and he
was as light skin as a piece of golden corn on the cob. he'd be
calling himself black and afrikan and upsetting everybody,
especially white people. they be calling him crazy but not to his
face. anyway the family, mainly the educated side, just left him
alone. they would just be polite to him, and every child of god
knows that when family members act polite, that means that they
don't want to be around you. it didn't matter much because after
his mother died he left the city and went into the army. the last
time we heard from him was in 1963. he got put out the army for
rioting. he disappeared somewhere between mississippi and
chicago. a third cousin, who family was also polite to, appeared
one day and said that luther had grown a beard, changed his
name and stopped eating meat. She said that he had been to

afrika and now lived in Chicago doing what he wanted to do, writing books, she also said that he smiles a lot and kinda got good teeth.

Findings

The Great Wait

(it is possible that those persons who feel the need
to act against evil will be told to wait, be calm,
have patience, don't get upset, be realistic, don't rock
the boat, you are not so bad off, etc., etc.)

conscious tire of
waiting on waiters who wait for a living
as movers perfect the reasons why
others must wait.

movers say that waiting is an ancient art form
perfected by negroes waiting on something called *freedom*

that will surely come
if the waiters wait patiently in the kneeling position long enough.
long enough is when the waiter's knees shine and
head automatically drops whenever waiters are in the presence
of movers that tell them to be grateful
to have something to wait for.

movers say that afrikans can't even clothe themselves,
that the major occupation in central america is the maintenance
  of cemeteries,
that the people of asia need to control their sex drive,
that the only people that *really* understand modern technology
are the south afrikaners and their brothers on pennsylvania
  avenue and
that the major problem for others is that they do not
want to wait for their time.

most of the waiters are poor and miseducated.
waiting, like cocaine, is addictive.
people wait on welfare, workfare, healthfare, foodfare,
and for businessmen and politicians to be fair.
waiters are line wise having spent a third of their lives
waiting in telephone lines, gas lines, light lines, bus lines,
  train lines, and unemployment lines.

waitin, waitin, tush, tush, tush.
waitin, waitin, tush, tush, tush.

waiters wait on presidents and first ladies to tell them
the secret of why waiting is better than
communism, socialism and hinduism,
why waiting is more uplifting than full employment
and is the coming tool to eliminate illiteracy and hunger.
waitin, waitin, tush.

western economist and sociologist have postulated that
waiting is the answer to family separations and ignorance.
that waiting will balance the budget and give waiters'
the insight into why others care more about their condition
than they do.

the conscious world
waits on a people who have become
professional waiters.
the waiters' education clearly taught them
to aspire to become either the
waiter, waitee or waited.
for most wasted
waitin, waitin, tush, tush, tush.
popular consensus has it that
waiting builds character, cures dumbness and blindness,
waiting brings one closer to one's creator, waiting is intelligent work,
waiting is the fat person's answer to
exercise
waiting will be featured on the johnny carson show this week
    disguised as
black urban professionals pushing the latest
form of waiting, "constructive engagement."
waitin, waitin, tush, tush, tush.
it is documented that
waiting will save the great whale population,
waiting will feed the children of the sudan,
waiting will stop acid rain,
waiting will save the great amazon rain forest,

waiting will guarantee disarmament and peace.
the major activity of waiters is watching television, sleeping, eating
junk foods and having frequent bowel movements.
waitin waitin tush tush tush tush

consciousness decays from
waitin on people with plastic bags
on their heads waitin
waitin on negroes that live for pleasure and money only waitin
waitin on a people that confuse freedom with handouts waitin
waitin on sam to straighten his spine and care for his children,
waiting on six child sue to say no,
waiting on $300 a day junkies,
waiting on a people whose heroes are mostly dead,
waitin on boldness from all this education we got,
waiting on the brother,
waiting on the sister.
waiting on waiters who wait for a living
as movers perfect the reasons why
others must wait.
waiting benefits non-waiters and their bankers.
most people are taught that
waiting is the misunderstood form of action,
is the act that is closest to sex and bar-b-q consumption.
waiting. waiting. waiting. waiting. waiting. waiting.
a truly universal art is practiced
by billions of people worldwide
who have been confirmed by their leaders
to be happy, satisfied and brain-dead.

negro: an updated definition part 368

for clarence pendleton and diana ross, to be read to the
popular song, "born in the USA"

negroes (negroes/knee grows) pc., -grows and devours itself;
invented around 1619 in the americas by the british, french,
spanish and portuguese. Also known as mulatto, creole, buck,
aborigine, quadroon, bitch, mixedblood, stud, half-breed, uncle
ben, aunt jemima, nigger and whatever.

BORN IN THE USA, THEY WAS BORN IN THE USA

negroes or treacherous and evil to own kind. major loyalty is to
anything, anybody lighter than black. hates the color of coal,
heats with gas or electricity, does not eat beans or fatback in
public, hides from watermelon and neckbones. the greens they
eat is spinach, and they dress in the fashion of calvin klein and
ann klein II. males are mostly clean shaved but are known to
wear mustaches. females shave legs and are known to throw-up at
the sight of dirt under fingernails.

BORN IN THE USA, THEY WAS BORN

possessors of designer jeans, license plates and minds. Negroes
have been bought and sold around the world with minimum
resistance. males and females are known to color their faces and
spend a good part of their days staring in mirrors and pressing
their heads. it is not unusual for them to have plastic surgery on
their mouths, noses and feet. during the early part of the century,
the males' necks were used to test the strength of ropes, and the
females were considered, except for pigs, the best breeders in the
world.

BORN IN THE

negroes live beyond their means and enjoy socializing with
people that don't like them. great gossipers and soap opera
enthusiasts. many run or jog from the word *racism*. politics gives
them headaches, and afrikan history is about as important as
country music. most bow and say sir to anything wearing a tie
and will die for country and general motors.

BORN

negroes live mainly in england, france, the carribean, united states, brazil and other places where europeans built churches, planted potatoes and put up barbed wire. The men die early and the women are alone most of the time, even when the men are alive. many are stock holders in mcdonalds and ibm and are lovers of cowboy and space movies.

THEY ARE BORN IN THE USA

negroes were reborn in such TV shows as *webster, gimme a break, the jeffersons, different strokes, benson, amen* and *miami vice.* they have currenlty captured the imagination of the world and hollywood in movies like *a soldier's story, the color purple* and *native son.* love money
more than self, love money more than self.
Negroes, the people that gave the world
billy dee williams and diahann carroll,
wake up and go to sleep praying,
"Thank God for Slavery."

THEY WERE MADE IN THE USA.

Seeking Ancestors

For the First Annual Egyptian Studies Conference, Los Angeles,
California, February 1984, organized by Maulana Karenga and
Jacob Carruthers

1.

what it was before death traps
before thriller and beat it, beat it
before soaps and reagan being raised to the station
of new redeemer by grandchildren viewing progress as
calvin klein & sonys in the ear.

where are the wise words,
the critical minds,
the questioners of sordid deeds,
the drinkers of pure water,
the doers of large moments?

what it was before emma lou planned her entire life
according to the stars & big sonny wilson hung on to every
syllable spoken by rev. ike, believe in me, and palm readers
from the pentagon?

what it is
is amnesia in america,
is memory the length of private parts,
is junk food masquerading as nutrition,
is projects and tenements replacing pyramids & space,
is fad posing as substance?

what it is
is strength measured by what you drink,
what you drive,
how you dress,
the texture of your hair
and the color of your woman,
"working hard for the money."

in america
working hard for the money
can get you bullets in the spine,
cocaine in the veins or a gold plated watch made in japan.
young death is guaranteed only if you think.
thinking in brazil & uganda,
in pakistan & south afrika is considered
contagious and dangerous.

shame and shock have evaporated.
grown men take their daughters and
boys hump boys and we are told that this
is modern, is normal, is in and in
america
where vacant heads copy & buy and
nourishment is derived from pepsis & cokes,
as vikings suck the blood of black people
draining the vision from the real miracles of the west
as we all approach the time when honor and integrity are obsolete
& preserved only in unread novels, unlistened music
as unattended grandmothers in michigan nursing homes
claim cats as family, friends and lovers.

2.

ever wonder where the circle came from
or who were the first people to use the triangle?
who were the original cultivators of the earth, who used
water of the nile to power minds and machines? what people
created music from instrument and voice and viewed the
building of cities as art and science? who were the
first to love because love contained the secrets of tomorrow?
look at yourselves.

there is magic in colors earthblack & purple issuing in
browns upon greens & oranges & others producing yellows
and ever present blue, skylike rain & water & warm.
today,
it is sure and dangerous to be dark in this universe.
there are secrets in color design,
there are mysteries in the making of the world,
there are complexities in the doings of strangers against the
    world.
there are clear courses that most minds are not ready for,
will never be able to perceive.
the west does serious damage to the mind.

america is not for sale, it is the buyer.

3.
we need clear language,
able storytellers,
discoverers of crops and seeds.
we need
decipherers and investigators of ideas & promise,
foreparents
screaming music that will arm us
with wisdom of the first,
warnings of
surrogate mothers and gene pool fathers.
we need
memory & moments, melody and song.
expanding vision
in search of winning ways and noble tomorrows.

comin back clearin eyes stompin, steppin, bolder
takin the wind & whispers seriously, takin the
slave beyond copy as cure, coping as necessity,
liftin the self & selves beyond rumor & wigs,
carrying the beauty of thought to completion,
knowing that if we think it,
doin it is only extension and reward
seekin to eclipse the expected to better & best.
if we have to beat it, beat it, try beatin the enemy,
try beatin those who reduced people to excretion & mannequins.

we were once music and might growin steel
we were beauty & find often feeling first drivin fire
we were seer & solution lift on up emma lou.
quiet step step
willinthefire, will in thefire, will in the fire
step step "dance to the music" step "dance to the music" step step
quiet and contemplative,
clearly conscious of wrongness
turn it around big sonny w. believe that
"we are family, my brothers, sisters & me."

4.

we conquered other selves in us
we became before we knew
tradition evaporated as others and many
stole the magic and wealth of millions.
diluting the dark people's walk & way,
cutting out the soul & source extricating the spirit
assassinating the common way.

Conquerors of vastness were
unable to copy lean steam
drumbeat walkers dancers carrying
spirit as gut & drive,
spirit as purpose and future
spirit as loving find,
as will & way
seeking beauty & meaning
in the secrets of ancient wall paintings
& buried souls.

5.
we are here
combat weary and willing
now & singing
looking special devoid of defeat
fired energy & hope imagining the inconceivable
here
urgently seeking lost records
igniting possibilities.

in the light of Amon and ancestors,
in the step of the clear and conscious,
it is beauty most needed in this place
as we recall that
by relinquishing building secrets

we lost clear water & children,
we lost future & wisdom & continuity.
we lost ourselves

demand
that the few & wise of us,
the monk & trane of us,
the careful & intelligent of us,
the hurston and dubois of us,
the silent and enduring of us,
the hansberry and woodson of us,
the conscious and loving of us,
to
recall the memory
to
recall the tradition & meaning
to rename the bringers
genius.
to quietly in the natural light of warm sunrises,
in the arms of loving smiles,
among the care of the consciously certain,
within the circle of the continued questioners,
to remember them ancestors all as

dark & talented.
as
gifted light
bringers of source,
bringers of silence,
bringers of remembrance.

ABOUT THE AUTHOR

An advocate of independent Black institutions, Haki R. Madhubuti is the founder, publisher and editor of Third World Press; founder and board member of the Institute of Positive Education/New Concept Development Center; and professor of English and director of the Gwendolyn Brooks Center at Chicago State University. He is a founding member of the National Black Wholistic Retreat Society and the Organization of Black American Culture. In 1990, he served on the National Commission on Crime and Justice.

Madhubuti received the African Heritage Studies Association's Community Service Award (1994), the American Book Award in 1991, and was named Author of the Year for the State of Illinois by the Illinois Association of Teachers of English (1991). He has been poet-in-residence at Cornell University, Howard University and Central State University. He is an active lecturer, community worker and researcher in the area of culture.

Madhubuti is currently the author of 19 books. He emerged on the literary scene in 1967 with the widely read *Think Black* and *Black Pride* (1968), and became recognized as one of the critical Black poets of the Sixties with the 1969 publication of *Don't Cry, Scream.* Haki Madhubuti's most recently published work is *Claiming Earth: Race, Rage, Rape, Redemption* which has received critical acclaim. His book, *Black Men: Obsolete, Single, Dangerous?* has sold in excess of 750,000 copies. His work has been highlighted on CBS's *Nightwatch*, National Public Radio's *All Things Considered*, the *Washington Post*, the *New York Times*, the *Chicago Tribune*, *Essence* magazine, *Black Entertainment Television*, *The MacNeil/Lehrer News Hour*, and the Chicago *Sun-Times*. He lives in Chicago with his wife and children.

ALSO AVAILABLE FROM THIRD WORLD PRESS

Nonfiction

*Million Man March/Day of
Absence: A Commemorative
Anthology: Speeches,
Commentary, Photography,
Poetry, Illustration and
Documents*
Edited by Haki R. Madhubuti
0-88378-188-3 Paper $19.95

Report From Part Two
by Gwendolyn Brooks
0-88378-162-X Paper $14.95

*Who Betrayed the African
World Revolution?*
by John Henrik Clarke
0-88378-183-2 Cloth $32.00
0-88378-136-0 Paper $14.95

*Testing African American
Students*
Edited by Asa G. Hilliard III
0-88378-152-2 Paper $14.95

*Infusion of African and
African American Content in
the School Curriculum*
Edited by Asa G. Hilliard III,
Lucretia Payton-Stewart, and
Larry Obadele Williams
0-88378-153-0 Paper $14.95

*Claiming Earth: Race, Rage,
Rape, Redemption
Blacks Seeking a Culture of
Enlightened Empowerment*
by Haki R. Madhubuti
0-88378-095-X Cloth $22.00
0-88378-090-9 Paper $14.95

*What is Life? Reclaiming the
Black Blues Self*
by Kalamu ya Salaam
0-88378-083-6 Paper $14.95

The Rap on Gansta Rap
by Bakari Kitwana
0-88378-175-1 Paper $5.95

*Lest We Forget: Howard
Beach and Other Racial
Atrocities*
by Alphonso Pinkney
0-88378-088-7 Paper $16.95

Approaches to Poetry Writing
by Keoropetse Kgositsile
0-88378-176-X Paper $5.00

*Life Sentences: Freeing Black
Relationships*
by Mzee Lasana Okpara
0-88378-146-8 Paper $8.00

*Warriors, Conjurers and
Priests: Defining African-
Centered Literary Criticism*
by Dr. Joyce Ann Joyce
0-88378-091-7 Cloth $29.95
0-88378-099-2 Paper $16.95

*African-Centered Education:
Its Value, Importance, and
Necessity in the Development
of Black Children*
by Haki R. Madhubuti and
Safisha Madhubuti Ph.D.
0-88378-151-4 Paper $5.00

Journey to Africa
by Hoyt W. Fuller
0-88378-018-6 Paper $8.95

*The Psychopathic Racial
Personality and other Essays*
by Bobby Wright
0-88378-071-2 Paper $5.95

Black Rituals
by Sterling Plumpp
0-88378-024-0 Paper $8.95

*In Search of Serenity: A
Black Family's Struggle with
the Threat of AIDS*
by Patti Renee Rose
0-88378-069-0 Paper $10.95

*The Redemption of Africa
and Black Religion*
by St. Clair Drake
0-88378-017-8 Paper $6.95

*Home is a Dirty Sreet: The
Social Oppression of Balck
Children*
by Useni Perkins
0-88378-048-8 Paper $6.95

*Harvesting New Generations:
The Positive Development of
Black Youth*
by Useni Perkins
0-88378-116-6 Paper $12.95

*Explosion of Chicago's Street
Gangs 1900 to Present*
by Useni Perkins
0-88378-017-8 Paper $6.95

*First Fruits: The Family
Guide to Celebrating
Kwanzaa*
by Imani A. Humphrey
0-88378-002-X Paper $7.95

The Black Anglo-Saxons
by Nathan Hare
0-88378-130-1 Paper $12.95

*Black Women, Feminism and
Black Liberation;Which Way?*
by Vivian Verdell Gordon
0-88378-111-5 Paper $5.95

*Focusing: Black Male-Female
Relationships*
by Delores P. Aldridge
0-88378-140-9 Paper $7.95

*Confusion by any Other
Name: Essays Exploring the
Negative Impact of The
Blackman's Guide to
Understanding the
Blackwoman*
Edited by Haki R. Madhubuti
0-88378-148-4 Paper $3.95

*Black Books Bulletin:
WordsWork: Blacks, Jews,
and Henry Louis Gates, Jr.*
Edited by Haki R. Madhubuti
Paper $6.00

How I Wrote Jubilee
by Margaret Walker
0-88378-025-9 Paper $1.50

Blackness and the Adventure
of Western Culture
by George Kent
0-88378-026-7 Paper $9.95

Reconstructing Memory
by Fred Hord
0-88378-144-1 Paper $12.95

New Plays for the Black
Theatre
Edited by Woodie King Jr.
0-88378-124-7 Paper $14.95

Poetry

Wise, Why's, Y's
by Amiri Baraka
0-88378-047-X Paper $12.00

Hornman
by Sterling Plumpp
0-88378-177-8 Paper $8.00

To the Bitter End
by Keorapetse Kgositsile
0-88378-082-8 Paper $8.00

Blacks
by Gwendolyn Brooks
0-88378-139-5 Cloth $36.95
0-88378-105-0 Paper $19.95

The Near-Johannesburg Boy
by Gwendolyn Brooks
0-88378-055-0 Paper $4.00

To Disembark
by Gwendolyn Brooks
0-88378-102-6 Paper $6.95

Poetry

Primer for Blacks
by Gwendolyn Brooks
0-88378-056-9 Paper $4.00

Very Young Poets
by Gwendolyn Brooks
0-88378-046-1 Paper $4.00

Winnie
by Gwendolyn Brooks
0-88378-050-X Paper $4.00

Don't Cry, Scream
by Haki R. Madhubuti
0-88378-016-X Paper $8.00

Killing Memory, Seeking
Ancestors
by Haki R. Madhubuti
0-88378-093-3 Paper $8.00

Earthquakes and Sunrise
Missions: Poetry and Essays
of Black Renewal
by Haki R. Madhubuti
0-88378-109-3 Paper $8.95

Mis Taken Brilliance
by Kahil El Zabar
0-88378-081-X Paper $8.00

The Present is a Dangerous
Place to Live
by Keoropetse Kgositsile
0-88378-057-7 Paper $8.00

Say that the River Turns:
The Impact of Gwendolyn
Brooks
by Haki R. Madhubuti
0-88378-118-2 Paper $8.95

Wings Will Not be Broken
by Darryl Holmes
0-88378-137-9 Paper $8.00

A Move Further South
by Ruth Miriam Garnett
0-88378-113-1 Paper $7.95

I've Been a Woman
by Sonia Sanchez
0-88378-112-1 Paper $7.95

Octavia and Other Poems
by Naomi Long Madgett
0-88378-121-2 Paper $7.95

Jiva: Telling Rites
by Estella Conwill Majozo
0-88378-138-7 Paper $8.00

So Far, So Good
by Gil Scott-Heron
0-88378-133-6 Paper $8.00

Manish
by Alfred Woods
0-88378-122-0 Paper $8.00

Elvis Presley is Alive and
Well and Living in Harlem
by Brian Gilmore
0-88378-004-6 Paper $8.00

Fiction

Maud Martha
by Gwendolyn Brooks
0-88378-061-5 Paper $9.95

The Brass Bed and Other
Stories
by Pearl Cleage
0-88378-127-1 Paper $8.00

The Future and Other Stories
by Ralph Cheo Thurmon
0-88378-125-5 Paper $7.95

The Sweetest Berry on the
Bush
by Nubia Kai
0-88378-059-3 Paper $8.00

Geechies
by Gregory Millard
0-88378-842-8 Paper $5.95

Young Adults and Children

The Afrocentric Self-Inventory
and Discovery Workbook for
African American Youth
by Useni Perkins
0-88378-043-7 Paper $5.95

The Story of Kwanzaa
by Safisha Madhubuti
Illustrated by Murray
DePillers
0-88378-001-1 Paper $6.95

Young Adults and Children

*Children of Africa: A
Coloring Book*
by The Drum and Spear
Collective
0-88378-076-3 Paper $5.95

*The Tiger Who Wore White
Gloves*
by Gwendolyn Brooks
Illustrated by Timothy Jones
0-88378-031-3 Paper $6.95

Black Fairy and Other Plays
by Useni Perkins
0-88378-077-1 Paper $13.95

I Look at Me
by Mari Evans
0-88378-038-0 Paper $2.50

*The Day They Stole the
Letter J
by Jabari Mahiri
Illustrated by Dorothy Carter
0-88378-084-4 Paper $3.95*